MATH 006

Nautical Custom

I0408858

Maritime Anthropology (MATH) a topic which covers prehistoric, historic and modern life, and inspirations derived from the world's oceans and the brave souls who have subsisted on and inhabited the surrounding environs of the sea.

MATH 006 Nautical Custom focuses on the rituals adhered to by maritime peoples, from appeasement of the gods, to superstitions, to legislature that affects life on the sea.

Research and module development

by

Yvonne-Cher Skye

Skye Research

Statement of Purpose

To create an educational program from which educators can create a program to sell to potential students as part of a maritime cultural experience. The intended audience can be variable from a one hour, one day seminar course to an 18 week course semester.

The actual lesson plans are at the discretion of the instructor. The materials available in this booklet are meant to be a reference point to assist the instructor in developing a foundation from which the intended course can be derived.

As this is in the early stages of production, all comments and suggestions for improvement are welcome.

Sincerely,

Yvonne-Cher Skye

Table of Contents

Summary

Objective:
Lecture on the topic of nautical customs, their origins, practice and modern developments.

Materials Needed:
Instructor: PowerPoint Presentation
Students: Journals, writing implements

Vocabulary introduced:
Bucentaur
Crossing the Line
To Flog a Dead Horse
Gerring of Grog
Traveling POSH

Background:

All of Maritime History began with the observation of the oceans and rivers by man.

Further specific lectures can be assigned module letters as the need arises.

Reference:
Seafaring Lore and Legend, Peter D. Jeans 2007
Wikipedia
Personal experiences
Personal research

Lesson Plan:
Introduce the terms and concepts via PowerPoint by using images and bulleted lists to convey the information. Dialogue with the students in a question and answer format.

Introduction:
Explain subject matter, and resource materials, with an eye on multimedia and hands-on instruction when materials are available.

Body:
Bucentaur
Crossing the Line
To Flog a Dead Horse

Gerring of Grog

Traveling POSH

Conclusion:

Direction on how instructor can conclude the module

Clean-Up:

Students take their things with them.

Learning sessions

Textbook reading chapters can be developed per the Instructor's chosen textbook or via their own manual dependent on scope of material intended to be covered in this course

Individual sections with dividers each focusing on one component of the content: All of the following will be determined by Instructor, module course outline gives examples of the following:

Learning outcomes

Session Information

Learning activities

Learning Resources

Evaluation Procedures

Timing and assignment

Course Outline

Catalog number: MATH 006   **Course Title:** Nautical Custom

Year: 2017   **Semester:** Spring

Instructor: **Office Location:**

Office Hours:

Objectives of the course:

> Explain nautical customs
>
> explain and identify military customs vs merchant customs
>
> explain and define nautical terminology
>
> Any measurable objectives that can be demonstrated by student
>
> Explain nautical occupations and duties ashore and aboard ship

Procedures for accomplishing these objectives:

> Lectures
>
> Class discussions
>
> Analytic questions
>
> Projects
>
> Research papers
>
> Use of visual and oral reports
>
> Fields trips
>
> Visiting lecturers
>
> Student testimonials
>
> Use of multimedia i.e. videos, audio recordings to exemplify topics

Student requirements for completion of the course:

> Varies per instructor discretion and length of program
>
> During introductory lecture, the instructor must list specific work students mustcomplete in order to receive credit for the course

Student need to demonstrate the accomplishment of each objective, examples are as follows:

Read all the chapters in the textbook

Submit a research paper

Oral report on topic

Submit book report

Complete lab reports

Complete periodic quizzes

Complete mid-term exam

Complete final exam

Grading Practices:

Students will be graded using above methods, at the instructor's discretion

Relative importance of each item

Four quizzes: 40%

Two book reports 20%

Term paper 20%

Final exam 20%

Equals 100%

Rules Concerning student absence and lateness:

At the discretion of the instructor and student agreement

If marina, ship or school follows specific rules, then state explicitly

Textbook:

List author, title publisher, date of publication of any required texts, manuals

Weekly Outline Topics to be covered:

List topics in sequential order

The Bucentaur

Crossing the Line

To Flog a Dead Horse

The Getting of Grog

Traveling POSH

Nautical Occupations

Duties of a nautical nature

Audio Visual Materials to be used:

List any visual elements to be used during course including:

PowerPoint presentations

Youtube videos

Photos

Graphs

Maps

List of supplementary readings:

MATH 006 Glossary

List books, periodicals, articles which students should read in addition to text

Miscellaneous information:

Any information that will further clarify what is hoped to be achieved in the course and how you plan to achieve it.

Audio Visual Experience

Photos

     Please see attached document entitled Photos.

     These will be updated as research is continued.

Useful weblinks leading to images can be found on the following websites:

Websites on subject

http://www.merriam-webster.com/dictionary/archetype

https://skyeresearchygfi.wordpress.com/2016/06/09/math-marine-anthropology-001-summary/

https://skyeresearchygfi.wordpress.com/2016/09/03/math-001-youtube-channel/

Audio recordings, videos or script to explain each section

Youtube channel Playlist MATH 001 at this link:

https://www.youtube.com/playlist?

list=PLBHbcZSn310CUhmMTkHoPqJlylPpYw1Jr

Appendices

Glossary

Maps

Artistic renderings

Works Cited

Glossary

A

Admiralty Law is the law of the sea.

Aid to Navigation is any fixed object that a navigator might use to find the vessel's position.

B

Bucentaur is the ceremony held on Ascension Day in Venice, when the state barge of Venice sails out to the bay, transporting the doge and other officials; who drop a ring into the Adriatic Sea to symbolize the city's ceremonial marriage to the Adriatic Sea.

C

certificate is any of the legal papers that identify the vessel, it's captain, and their licenses.

chart datum is the water level referenced when recording data on a chart; it is a given average for a region.

charter is the act of renting a boat from an individual, company or a marina for a specified length of time.

Close – up is when the flag that is hoisted to the top of a flag pole.

close-winded is when the vessel is able to sail close to the direction of the wind.

Colors is the national flag or other flags that are flown on a vessel.

Courtesy flag is a smaller version of the flag of a country that is flown when one is visiting said country.

cowtailing is when the lines of a strand begins fraying when the strands have become unlaid.

crew is the collective term which defines the individuals who function aboard a ship and on the docks who assist in the tasks and duties that enable a boat to function successfully.

Crossing the Line is a ceremony that commemorates a sailor's first crossing of the equator.

D

danger zone for a powerboat, the section from dead ahead to two points abaft the starboard beam, in which approaching powerboats have the right of way

ditty bag was formerly a sailor's personal repair kit, with needles, thread, buttons and other articles; while today it is a boat's repair kit, with sail-mending materials, sail tools, cotter pins, tape and other articles.

E

Ensign is the American Flag, which is flown on all American Vessels.

F

fairway is an open channel in which all manner of vessels may sail.

fid is a round, tapered hardwood spike used to open up strands in lines or rope, to prepar them for splicing.

fixed light is a light that displays a constant, unchanging color to act as a navigational aid; the color and flashing of the light are all indicators of a specific meaning.

flashing is the mode of a light of not more than 30 regular flashes per minute, with each flash shorter than the period of darkness

flat seam is a common stitch used to sew together overlapping pieces of cloth.

Found means equipped as in a well-found boat; meaning that all attributes necessary for a ship to function in it's assigned tasks.

full-and-by is sailing a vessel close-hauled.

G

Give-way vessel is the vessel that in a given scenario when two or more vessels meet; it does not have the right-of-way.

GMT means Greenwich Mean Time; which is a universally agreed upon hence coordinated universal time is a newer standard a time standard that is not affected by time zones or seasons

Green buoy is a can buoy; which is a navigational aid.

Green daymark is a navigational aid used in U.S. and Canada mark a channel Green triangular daymark should be kept on the left when returning from a larger to a smaller body of water, Red day marks mark the other side of the channel

H

hail is the attempt to contact another boat or shore, by voice or radio

hand is the title of someone who helps with work on a boat; sometimes named a crew member.

handsomely is to perform a task, or say a statement in a careful and proper manner.

handy-billy is a moveable block and tack

harbor master is an individual who responsible for a harbor, its customs, laws, and procedures.

hard-a-lee is a spoken command given to the helmsman to steer a boat downwind.

Hazard is an object that may prevent the safe operation of a vessel.

herringbone stitch is a stitch used to sew together the edges of a rip, in which each stitch pulls together the edges and holds them fast.

hiking is the leaning of a vessel far out to windward to offset heeling

I

International code of signals is a set of radio, sound and visual signals designed to aid in communications between vessels to bypass a language problem. Morse code, signal pennants, spoken code letters are all examples.

Isobars are lines drawn on a weather map indicating regions of equal pressure. Close together with rapid change and strong winds

K

Knot is a speed of one nautical mile per hour

L

Lead is a weight used for sounding depths, usually hollow on one end to permit arming, so as to pick up a sample of the bottom

Lee bowing the current is to sail with the current on the lee bow which enables the boat to make good a course closer to the wind than she is actually steering.

Left rudder is a command to the helmsman to steer the boat to the left.

licensed pilot is an individual who has licenses and qualified to guide vessels in a particular area.

lie is 1. where an object is located. 2. to put an object in place.

Life jacket is a devices that keep one afloat; life preserver or personal flotation device (PFD), life vest.

Liquid petroleum gas (LPG) is propane that is preferred over regular fuel for cooking and heating aboard ship.

lookout is the individual who watches for other vessels and hazards.

M

make fast is the act of attaching a line securely to a surface or an item so that it won't move.

make way is the act of moving through the water

marina is a place where boats can find fuel, water, other services, and rent slips where boats can dock.

mayday is an internationally recognized distress signals used on a radio to indicate a threatening situation these calls have priority once any other radio transmissions and should only be used if immediate threat to life or vessel

Mediterranean berth is a method of docking with the boats tied with their stern at the dock.

moor is the act of attaching a boat to a mooring dock, post, or anchor.

mooring is a place where a boat is moored, whether to buoy marks, with the vessel's location firmly set to anchor.

Morse Code A is a short-long flashing signal showing a short flash of about .4 seconds followed by an eclipse of the same length.

Motorboat is any boat under 65 feet long propelled by machinery, except tugboats and towboats propelled by steam.

N

navigation rules are the marine traffic rules observed and maintained by the United States Coast Guard, covering both Inland and International Waters.

no-sail zone is the zone where a sailboat can not sail. It tends to be 90 degrees wide, with the center point being directly toward the true wind direction

Nun buoy is a navigational aid, that is a cone-shaped buoy; usually painted red, bearing an even number, and marking the starboard side of the channel when entering from seaward.

O

on beam ends is when a vessel is heeled over so far that the the boat's deck beams are vertical.

on the wind is when a vessel is sailing close-hauled.

out of trim is when the sails of a vessel are not properly arranged for the point of sail that the boat is on the sails way be luffing or have improper sail shape, or the boat may be heeling too much. These conditions will slow the boat down.

overtaking is when a vessel is approaching from more than two points abaft the beam

overtrimmed is a condition when sheets are hauled in too close for sails to capture the full power of the wind

owner's flag is a boat owner's private pennant which is flown when at sail or at dock.

P

Palm and needle whipping is a permanent sewn binding on the end of a line, finished with worming to hold the turns of the whipping secure.

pan-pan is an emergency message used to signal when a vessel is in trouble similar to mayday.

passengers are those individuals who have no part in working the boat.

Payout is to let out a line, to ease off, or give more slack

pennant is 1. a small signal flag, spells words. 2. a small line attached to the mooring

piling is the support post for a pier.

Pilot is the individual who has specific knowledge of a harbor, canal, river, other waterways who is qualified to guide a vessel through the region

plain whipping is a temporary binding on the end of a line, in which both ends of the binding twine are buried in the whipping

point is a sail as close as possible to the wind an 25 degree arc of the horizon

pole lift is a topping lift.

port tack is sailing with the wind coming over the port side, the sails are set to starboard.

privileged vessel is a stand on vessel required to maintain course and speed when two boats are approaching one another

Q

Quarantine flag is a pennant flown when entering a country indicating that the people on the ship are healthy and that the vessel wants permission to visit the country. As opposed to the skull and crossbones which indicated unhealthy conditions aboard the ship.

Quick-stop method is a man overboard rescue technique in which you instantly stop the boat to enable crew to be as close to the victim as possible

R

Range lights are two white lights carried by steam vessels one forward and low, the other aft and high to make courses changes apparent.

Ratlines are small lines tied between shrouds to use as a ladder when a crew member or the captain must go aloft

Reaching is sailing across the wind; or wind going across the boat, any heading or direction. sailing across the wind; it is the point of sailing between close-hauled and running.

Reef knot is a square knot, an unreliable knot used to loosely tie lins @ the bundles of sail

Reef points are 1. several horizontal points where lines have been attached to ties the extras sail out of the way after reefing

Regatta is a series of races with the cumulative race scores counting for the final residues

Relative bearing is measured in degrees with the cumulative race scores counting for the final results 2. the bearing of an object measure from ahead in relation to the boat's centerline from 0 degrees clockwise to 360 degrees.

Rig is to prepare a boat for use.

Rigger's knife is a knife fitted with a cutting blade and a marlinespike

Right of way is the legal right of a vesel to continue course and speed when in a meeting situations, the right to maintain course and speed in a situation where danger of collision exists.

Right rudder is a command to the helmsman to steer the boat to the right.

Round seam is a stitch that binds together two edges of cloth, leaving a rough welt on one surface.

Rules of the Road –are the rules of conduct which concerns which vessel has the right of way when there is a possibility of collision

Running is the course the helmsman is steering when the wind is behind them.

Running Bowline is a knot that tightens under load. Formed by running that standing line through loop formed in a regular bowline.

Running lights that are on a boat that is required by law to be shown between sundown and sunup or times of limited of visibility.

S

Scope is the 1. ratio between depths of water and anchor rope. 3:1 is minimum for anchoring in protected water and scopes up to 7:1 are recommended in exposed conditions

Sculling is the propelling a boat forward by working and twisting the blade of an oar from side to side over the boat's stern

Scuttlebutt is gossip

Seaman's Eye is the ability to judge a boat's carrying and shooting qualities under varying conditions of wind and sea.

Secure is to make fast; slow an object, or tie in place

Seize is to fasten together or bind by lashing

Semaphore is when the use of two flags held in position by a flagger.

She is the manner in which all boats are referred to as female.

Shipshape means to be in clean, orderly condition

Short splice is a splice used to join together two lengths of line of the same diameter by "marrying" their ends and interweaving their strands. It increases the line's diameter.

Skipper is the person in command of a boat the captain

Splice is to permanently join 2 ropes by tucking strands of each over the other, creating a smoother joint than any knot

Spring Line is docking lines that help keep the boat from fore and aft while docked

Stand-on vessel is the one having the right of way

Standing line is the main part of a line; part not used in a knot

Steam vessel is any vessel propelled by machinery.

Stopper knot is a knot used on the end of a line to prevent the end from running through a block or other narrow space prevents a line that slips from unthreading and getting lost

Strike means to lower

Swinging bridge is a bridge that swings away from the water wasy so that boats may pass by it

T

tall buoy; dan buoy is a float with a flag at the top of a pole used to mark a position such as for a race or a man overboard.

To Flog a Dean Horse means to waste energy or thoughts on a lost cause or unalterable situation.

Traveling POSH means port out starboard home, a preferred form of travel in the 1890's for ships traveling from England and India.

tuck is in a splice, one round of interweaving of the strands of the working end into the strands of the standing part, also to interweave

Two half hitches are knots 2 loop on standing part of a line

U

Underway is when a vessel is in motion and not at anchor.

USCG is an acronym for the United States Coast Guard

W

watch is the division of crew into shifts. 2) time each watch has duty

weather helm is the tendency of a boat to head up towards the eye of the wind opposites of lee helm

whipping a binding usually of waxed sail twine, put on the ends of line or rope to keep the strands from unlaying

wide berth is a method used to avoid something by a large distance

wing and wing is running before the wind with two sails set; running with jib set on one side and mainsail on the other.

wing the jib is when sailing on a run, to trim the jib on the opposite side as the mainsail

worming is a small line in the connections of a stranded line or rope.

Works Cited

http://www.merriam-webster.com/dictionary

Maps

will be added per the request and special requirements of the instructor.

Artistic renderings

will be added per the request and special requirements of the instructor.

Works Cited

http://www.merriam-webster.com/dictionary

Back Page

For further sources and information on the research conducted on this topic, it is recommended that you order the supplemental materials entitled notes and photos.